Acknowledgemen...

The author is grateful to the editors of the following books and journals, where some of these poems first appeared:

Breath & Shadow - A Journal of Disability Culture and Literature, "Stones and Hard Edges," "Lost," "Waiting for the Fullness of Time"

Wordgathering, "I Wanted To See," "They Live," "Impish Blues"

The Berkshire Review, "One Voice, Then Two"

Inglis House Poetry Workshop Chapbook *their buoyant bodies respond*, "To Sing the Children Home"

Inglis House Poetry Workshop Chapbook *Bone & Tissue*, "Rolling Backwards"

Lifting Women's Voices: Prayers to Change the World (a Morehouse publication), "Spread Wings and Fly"

The Episcopal Church and the Visual Arts, "A Pentecost Day"

Sandcutters, The Arizona State Poetry Society, "et lux perpetua luceat eis"

In The Crayon Box, There Is Peace

Poems

Judith Krum

For Randy

"my well-spring in the wilderness"

George Eliot [Mary Ann Evans]

"The Spanish Gypsy"

"But what have I, but what have I, my friend,

To give you, what can you receive from me?"

T.S. Eliot

"Portrait of a Lady"

Contents

In the Crayon Box, There is Peace   1

one..

Footprints and Dusty Whispers   3

Among the Streets and Alleys of the Poor   4

Rags and Bare Feet   5

How Sweet and Fitting   6

What Was It Like Before?   7

Collisions   8

In the Andalusian Sunlight   9

Spread Wings and Fly   10

What Happens if a Stranger Says Hello?   11

Asphalt Recesses   12

Sunlight Burnished   13

In the Square Tiled Rooms   14

two..

The Earth Will Be Asking   16

Waiting for the Fullness of Time   17

One Voice, Then Two   18

Impish Blues   19

The Pulse of Summer   20

The Nectar of the Rose   21

The Silent Scent of Hyacinths   22

Amethyst and Aubergine   23

The Arrogant Aspen   24

A Pentecost Day   25

A Thousand Scarlet Tulips   26

Like Florins Lost   27

The Eyes of Winter   28

Take This Hope of a Day   29

three..**....**

Stones and Hard Edges   *31*

Fragments of Scotch   *32*

Vestiges   *33*

Carry Bags   *34*

Riding the Roof's Ridge   *35*

et lux perpetua luceat eis   *36*

Words Unraveled   *38*

Now the Back Page   *39*

To Sing the Children Home   *40*

The High School Memorial Reunion   *41*

No Ripeness There   *42*

Rolling Backwards   *43*

four...

Dottie's Diner   *45*

On the Tip of My Tongue   *46*

The Game   *47*

Battle Zucchini   *48*

Myrtle the Turtle　49

Sorry　50

Abigail, the Dueña of the Frigidaire　52

Wonder Where They Went　53

The Diva　54

They Live　55

five...

My Grandfather Had Mahogany Fingers　57

Bas Relief　58

Smoking Her Chesterfields　59

Your Next Email　61

I See On Facebook　62

The Ballad of Stitches and Schemes　63

Lost　65

I Wanted to See　66

I Will Put You In A Poem　67

To See You in the Shadows　68

When I Have Loved Enough　69

In the Crayon Box, There Is Peace

"the poet's duty: whose voice helps mankind endure and prevail"
William Faulkner, 1950 Nobel Lecture

In the crayon box
Razzle Dazzle Rose lies beside Radical Red.
Atomic Tangerine and Unmellow Yellow
    share the same half inch of cardboard territory.
Wild Blue Yonder knows that it is part of the same family
    as Purple Heart and Desert Sand.
The crayons are a mix
    of old and new, sharp and smooth, pointy and dull.
The inside of the box is spotted with dots of color,
    Optically intermingled,
    Like Seurat's pointillism,
    Bringing out a more vivid impression
    When viewed as an entirety.
These myriad hues have blended into a synthesis
    of peaceful coexistence.
    Chartreuse is no more important than Olive Green.
    Flamingo Pink is no more beautiful than Wild Watermelon.
    Purple Mountain's Majesty takes up no more space
    than Tropical Rain Forest.
In the crayon box, there is peace.

one...

Footprints and Dusty Whispers

They surprise me,
    the people who live in the woodwork of my life.
They emerge from the baseboards unexpectedly
    and rouse me to remember
The Ivory soap I used and the soft Wonder bread.
They unearth silhouettes and shadowy figures,
    the student loved and the friend now dead.
They revive the lost and the chosen,
    the desired and the abandoned.
They reveal a legacy of children and books,
    watercolors and pottery.
From the casements of my dwelling places,
    they show me the houses that have been sold
    with new bathrooms and open kitchens.
Mortise and tenon joinery holds us together
    in spite of farewells and moving vans.
They astonish me,
    the people that rise from the woodwork of my life.
They furnish the attic of my years
    with comfy chairs and flowered wallpaper,
    with thick albums of Kodak prints,
    with unchanged voices and toddler hand prints.
My woodwork residents do not herald their coming
    with trumpets and fanfares.
No, they arrive secretly, leaving their footprints in sawdust
    and their dusty whispers in the wind.

3

Among the Streets and Alleys of the Poor

To seek some meaning and to find my core,
I turn to find the conscience of my days
Among the streets and alleys of the poor.

I search the length of sadness, tears, and war
As living takes its toll. I cannot find the ways
To seek some meaning and to find my core.

Sometimes I cannot bear to see one more:
The children's tears, the broken lives, clichés
Among the streets and alleys of the poor.

I listen for the songs, block out the roar
Of heartache and the depth of dark malaise
To seek some meaning and to find my core.

The covenant I have makes me deplore
The tortured, agonized and bent displays
Among the streets and alleys of the poor.

My soul is searching legends, stories, lore,
In hopes of finding vision worth the praise,
To seek some meaning and to find my core
Among the streets and alleys of the poor.

Rags and Bare Feet

If beauty's truth and truth is beauty,
Where do we find
The greatest splendor,
The most unsuspecting honesty?
Dog's paws, clotheslines, and petunias,
Grandmother's aprons, safety pins, nameless heroes,
Jars of pennies and Caribbean sunsets.
'Beauty's best in unregarded things,'
Said Lowell to Miss D.T.
The golden mean of harmony and balance:
There must be truth in rags
And beauty in bare feet.

How Sweet and Fitting

A poet's work is to name the un-nameable, to point at frauds, to take sides, start
arguments, shape the world, and stop it going to sleep. ~ Salman Rushdie

Shelley penned that 'nothing beside remains.'
And on the urn, Keats birthed the marble men and maidens,
'Who are these coming to the sacrifice?'
Auden said 'the question is absurd'
And rearranged their names to Kelly and Sheets
While turning the tables with irony and grace.
'The ignorant armies gathered in the night,' said Arnold,
And Auden, like Yeats, cursed Adam,
As he wrote his lines, bereaved,
with signs of sadness, deep unease.
When trouble strained the peace, he fell down on his knees.
Auden rallied with the thinkers and the poets, deeply grieved,
With Arnold and with Owen, with Eliot and Sassoon,
No joy, nor hope, nor love in the 'now late afternoon.'
With Housman, too, he "knew the creeds outworn,"
The unrelenting greatness and the merciless sense of words.
"If anything was wrong, we should certainly have heard."
The poets of the past looked grievously dismayed.
They took apart the myths that once were known as truth,
And now we're left with just the skin and flesh, no pith.
The cups, the marmalade, the tea. Eat a peach. Do I dare?
"Dulce et decorum est, pro patria mori."

What Was It Like Before?

What was it like before, before the pain,
Before the purple bruises and the games.
What was it like before, when we were sane,
Had common sense, not fabricated claims.

There was a time before when no one cried,
When no one pointed, screaming, "Let them die."
When we had names, we took enormous pride
In helping those who struggled. We would try

To move huge mountains and restore the reign
Of common sense. We need to find those ways
To meet the basic needs of those who strain
To live their lives in better, sun-filled days.

If not, all smiles and laughter soon will cease,
And coffins lined with purple will increase.

Collisions

The River Lethe lulls soundless souls to sleep
So night can crown forgetfulness the king.
The masks of gray all slip into the deep,
But dawn awakes to show what day will bring.
The gold of sun, the azure blue of sky,
And green and tan spread out on earth's expanse -
These colors paint a scene we can't deny
As day bursts forth to show us how, perchance,
Our living and our dying settle in
To give us rainbow colors that provide
The bumps and bruises on our day's thin skin.
Life shows us how our hopes and dreams collide.
Our living, then, jolts us with such surprise
That changes, good and bad, can death disguise.

In the Andalusian Sunlight

Blood trickles over the yellow grains in the *albero*,
pulsing rivulets like arteries through the sand.
Anticipating his date with death,
the matador grips the scarlet *muleta*
and readies for the final *suerte*.
He studies the bull as it paws the ground with its forefeet,
sending dirt flying behind it,
and blowing angry breath from its nostrils.
The matador tips his *montera* to the President,
and the *tendido* roars as the bull shakes his *pitones*.
The matador's suit of lights sparkles in the Andalusian sunlight
at four in the afternoon.
His ivory silk jacket, heavily embroidered with gold,
like an embellished chausable sewn for Easter mass,
hugs his body like a second skin.
The matador's pink stockings, already spotted
with the blood of the bull, wrinkle around his ankles
and catch some yellow sand in the folds.
Fanning the *muleta* close to his body, the matador breathes heavily
to ignite the bull's determination
while the *pasadobles* sound above the crowd's roar.
The matador scans his own demons
through eyes narrowed into slits
as the red cape barely whirls by the bull's side with a flourish.
For the final act of the *faena*,
three more sinuous unfurlings of the cape
and then the signal from the President.
The matador delivers the fatal thrust, the *estocada*.
With the waving of the white handkerchiefs,
the crowd signals its approval
of the matador's disdainful artistry
and the graceful avoidance of his own death.
The gold embroidery of the matador's sequined jacket
shimmers in the fading Andalusian sunlight
at the tolling of the bell
at five in the afternoon.
The President awards the ears.

Spread Wings and Fly

To cure, to heal, to live, to love? Profound.
For legs to work, and hands to grasp, arms hold,
For eyes to see and ears to catch the sound,

For body parts all working and not cold.
We let some bodies feel the chill and ice,
As hearts are once again so strongly told

To keep away. The loving pay the price
And join the throng to be a tiny part
Of that unending, blessed sacrifice

That lifts the fading spirit. Oh, please impart
The spark that brings the soul and sacred heat
To ice-encrusted, fragile, brittle heart.

The candles lit, the meal prepared, we greet
The ones who, singing antiphons, stand tall.
We dare not shun and pass as incomplete

The ones who cannot speak or give a call
Or those who laugh and shout and, tearless, cry
With hands and arms that do not make a wall.

Lord, do not let us give away a sigh
But help us love, lift up, spread wings, and fly.

What happens if a stranger says hello?

All along the street I walk in snow.
My shoes are thin; my feet are wet and cold.
What happens if a stranger says hello?

The way winds on until right there, just so,
I see the darkened house all still. It's sold.
All along the street I walk in snow.

The bricks are rough and red, a bleak tableau.
The windows dark with shades all blackened, rolled.
What happens if a stranger says hello?

I cannot see beyond the walls, although
With thoughts of light and life, I am consoled.
All along the street I walk in snow.

As snow begins again to fall, I know
I will no longer see where I have strolled.
What happens if a stranger says hello?

My feet are dragging, and my steps are slow.
Fear and dark conspire to deepen cold.
All along the street I walk in snow.
What happens if a stranger says hello?

Asphalt Recesses

Like cousins you see only once a year,
The miles fly by and disappear
Into scrapbooks and photo albums.
You can scarcely remember the names
Or the time or the place or the reason.
The miles resonate a past time
When car trips carried whole families
From one Burma Shave sign to the next.
Even now the miles race by.
Faces are washed in gray white shadows
Like the blur between electric poles.
All type set and pencil-colored on a Rand McNally map,
The concrete interstates merge into blacktopped country roads,
Soft and sticky in the summer heat. The roads
Suck you down into asphalt recesses
Where the miles slow down
So you can see your cousins' faces
And smell the road in your hair.

Sunlight Burnished

daybreak
opens the day
stretches arms toward light
gray blue skies peek through the window
cloudless

morning
brings sunrise bright
daffodil wakings
upon saffron threads of sunbeams
rising

daytime
bronze for working
toil treads on ruddy paths
muscles strain in goldenrod heat
effort

evening
fuchsia descends
below the red sunset
streams of crimson, amethyst, pink
wonder

midnight
breathes coolness
starry air glints sparkles
twinkles flash, spangles spark and shine
burnished

daybreak
brings sunrise bright
toil treads on ruddy paths
streams of crimson, amethyst, pink,
burnished

In the Square Tiled Rooms

Down the tiled hallway past one room and the next,
      the sun goes through an open door and disappears.
In one square tiled room,
      the occupant's breath, like sand at high tide,
      is flattened by the moon.
And in the next square tiled room,
      the lodger has paid his rent and lies patiently waiting,
      his slippers beside the bed.
And in the next square tiled room
      a visitor sits in a bentwood oak chair at the foot of the bed,
      listening to the air whooshing through the slit
      in the blue vinyl seat cushion.
When he rises to go to the next square tiled room,
      he can't lift his feet high enough
      to climb over the door sills.
Dragging his feet through golden pools,
      he makes waves and rivulets
      in the syrupy, whispered prayers.
It's like slogging through treacle.

two..

The Earth Will Be Asking (Gloss)

"Inversnaid"
Gerard Manley Hopkins

What would the world be, once bereft
Of wet and of wildness? Let them be left,
O let them be left, wildness and wet;
Long live the weeds and the wilderness yet.

What would the world be, once bereft
Of sorrel and speedwell and mistletoe and dock?
Of zebra and lions and flocks of woodcock?
Will highways and buildings, will asphalt and blocks
Be all that remain amid concrete and rocks?
What would the world be, once bereft

Of wet and of wildness? Let them be left
For the times when our children will ask to be set
With acres for roaming and tall birch minarets.
The earth will be asking the why and just get
The moaning of eons and cries of 'not yet',
Of wet and of wildness? Let them be left

O let them be left, wildness and wet
Like the great ocean reefs and whitecaps that break,
The fast running rivers and deltas that make
The homes for the gators, the turtles and drakes.
The brooks and the springs, the creeks and the lakes,
O let them be left, wildness and wet

Long live the weeds and the wilderness yet.
Remove the barbed wire, the fences and hedge,
Bring back the prairie, the falls, and the sedge,
The oaks and the pine woods so robins can fledge.
And eagles can soar high above the earth's edge.
Long live the weeds and the wilderness yet.

Waiting for the Fullness of Time

Round and firm, the peas wait inside their shells.
When unzipped, the waxy pods will
Squeak and surrender their delights
Jingling into the footed metal colander below -
Within reach, but not quite ready.

Under festoons of spider webs
Luscious purple grapes hang in the arbor.
Juicy sweetness
Just waiting to fill oaken barrels -
Will be, but not just yet.

Cucumber vines creep along the ground
Sending roots down and tendrils up.
Trellises and fences support the fruits -
Smooth and nubby, green and striped -
Waiting for brine and spices -
Almost, but not quite.

One Voice, Then Two

The fanfare in the skies tells us they're here.
The beating wings keep rhythm with the heart.
The geese are flying north again this year.

Cast in their V, they suddenly appear.
We stop, look up, unable to depart.
The fanfare in the skies tells us they're here.

One voice, then two, then scores dispel the drear
From souls too long without their grace and art.
The geese are flying north again this year.

Their bodies glide, their necks thrust out, austere.
In them we see what air and sun impart.
The fanfare in the skies tells us they're here.

The trumpets and the flourish of our sphere,
The call, the swell of wings, our counterpart.
The geese are flying north again this year.

Their need is flight, the freedom but to steer
Their lives each spring along time's unknown chart.
The fanfare in the skies tells us they're here.
The geese are flying north again this year.

Impish Blues

Forget-me-nots announce the birth of spring.
Tiny blue jumbles in the young grass, not yet mowed.
Sprigs and spurts of pint-sized periwinkle
Run amok in tufts of green.
Creeping roots explore the lawn with great abandon.
Mischievous forget-me-nots refuse to be tidy.
They will not be neatly arranged.
They cannot be artfully composed.
They do not respond to the name
'Myosotis Alpestris.'
They are not named Elizabeth or Margaret,
But Betsy and Peggy.
Cousin to cowslips and heliotropes,
These impish blues jump in puddles
And arrive at the party with mud on their shoes.
With bonnets all tangled,
They ignore the brick edges of the garden path,
And, following their own tiny way,
Their mouse-ear blue petals skip toward the sapphire sky.

The Pulse of Summer

I watch the pulsing waves of heat that rise
Above the rolling hills and greening haze,
Across the deep blue teal and cloudless skies
While summer strolls along the line of days.

Above the rolling hills and greening haze
My summer blood gives way to warmth divine.
While summer strolls along the line of days,
I find the sunflowers, daisies, columbine.

My summer blood gives way to warmth divine.
With heady scents of sweat and sweet and musk,
I find the sunflowers, daisies, columbine
And follow freeform days to lazy dusk.

With heady scents of sweat and sweet and musk,
My summer flowers mix with earthy smells
And follow freeform days to lazy dusk.
The sun will set amid the soft pastels.

My summer flowers mix with earthy smells
While days flow on to birth the fragrant rose.
My sun will set amid the soft pastels
As my summer ambles on to find its close.

The Nectar of the Rose

Along the petals of the sweetest rose
Love's nectar drips, that aromatic mist that flows
Along the drifting days, not to delay
Summer's sweet and rapturous repose.

The rose so freely gives its scent away,
Transmitting rich perfume throughout the day,
While nettle, sage and milkweed all direct
Their wild pungence to a mock bouquet.

And as my youthful, summer days protect
Me from that bitter nosegay, I reflect
Upon the ways my life has paid so dear
With losses, tears, and friendships circumspect.

When summer breezes bring the sweetness here
And dazzling blossoms finally appear,
I know that time will soon exhale a sigh
For yet another unpretentious year.

A rosey sunset will enhance the sky
While damask roses piled up so high
Will try to cover up the gloomy pall,
That pain of days that comes to say goodbye.

Those are the whiffs of memoir's incense ball,
A lover's final words I did recall,
Not rose-inspired, tantalizing scent,
But potions made of sweat and tears and gall.

When all the misery of life's torment
Turns round about and gives its last assent,
There's nothing left except the scent that flows
From petals of the rose's last lament.

Maundy Thursday
The Silent Scent of Hyacinths

"If I had but two loaves of bread, I would sell one and buy hyacinths, for they would feed my soul." (Prophet Muhammad, 570-632)

Drawn to this room by hyacinths so sweet,
The heady fragrance soothes the aching soul.
We drink the silent scent of prayer complete.

We make this shrouded space a white retreat
For Body, pure, to comfort and console.
Drawn to this room by hyacinths so sweet,

We bare our souls, and thus we so entreat
Our plea for humble access to the goal.
We drink the silent scent of prayer complete.

Sotto voce, speak the truth discrete
And beg the heart to forfeit its control.
Drawn to this room by hyacinths so sweet,

We fear the candlelight will be too fleet.
We climb the hill to see the darkened knoll.
We drink the silent scent of prayer complete.

The sky splits wide; the lightning shrieks defeat.
Could you not wait for all to take the toll?
Drawn to this room by hyacinths so sweet,
We drink the silent scent of prayer complete.

Amethyst and Aubergine

From the kaleidoscope of colors at the store
I picked the finest color I could find
To paint the Floria Emporia,
My bloom-filled, petal-loving marketplace.
The periwinkle paint dressed the décor.
The hue was lush and dense and so designed
To give a sense of wild euphoria.
And then, to lilacs in a thistle vase,
I added iris, orchids, phlox galore.
They made a fragrant bouquet, all combined
With perfumed garland of wisteria
Festooned about my morning glory space.
My royal purple shop will be the scene
For ritual meant for me, the flower queen,
With crown of amethyst, robe of aubergine.

The Arrogant Aspen

"That of this tree the Cross was made, which erst the Lord of glory bore" -
Anon., 'The Aspen'

On that fateful Friday, known as Good,
Trees shuddered in the shadows,
As the dark encompassed the world.
Fluttering leaves, like Irish women keening,
Trembling,
Rocking,
Carried that woeful cry to the stars and back again.
The air was cold with quivering;
Icy notes swaying the clapping chorus of ullaloo.
But one tree, the Aspen tree,
Refused to bend its branches
In deferential genuflection,
And was made to quake perpetually,
To twitch its arrogant branches
In the slightest breeze,
And rattle its tremulous leaves,
Creating chatter like the tongues of malicious gossipers.
It would never know quiet
Nor peace again,
That Friday that was Good,
That quaking keening,
That fateful darkness.

A Pentecost Day

A Pentecost Day -
The sun's shaft sent tongues of fire
 through the shadows of the trees,
Painting red and gold bright
 with the expectation of heavenly bliss.
The wind wound its way through the leaves,
 dancing branches quivering with hopeful anticipation.
Like people reaching their final purpose,
 after lives lived long and hard,
 the leaves marched in procession
 behind the banner of the Dove,
 the spirit of newness and hope.
A Pentecost Day.

A Thousand Scarlet Tulips

(from an ancient Persian legend)

Each drop of blood the sign of Farhad's love
For Shirin; each red tulip formed like lips
That never more the Persian youth would move.
The morning light revealed the rounded tips,
The waxy petals, each encircling each
Like sculpted arms around an aching heart.
His horse had hurled him far across the breach,
This youth, Farhad, who would not be apart
From his desire, so pure, so true. And down
He plunged, and from his blood the tulips grew,
A thousand scarlet tulips, each a crown
For such lost love. With painfilled tint imbue
Those crimson turbans all across the lands
To show young lovers what such love demands.

Like Florins Lost

When winter blasts throughout the forest floor,
The leaves of autumn scatter one last time,
Like florins lost to pirates and to lore,
Those treasured gold doubloons that clink and chime.

The forest floor becomes a carpet gold
That shimmers in the splinters of last light.
The golden leaves, rare bullion, can't be sold
Or bartered for another year's delight.

No, finally the winter's wind swirls round
And captures all the coinage left behind,
Creating leaf-lined graves on waiting ground
As numismatic blasts keep gold confined.

The gold turns into darkness, shrouding sun,
As autumn's leaves are once again undone.

The Eyes of Winter

The eyes of winter squint against the cold,
The cold that burns its icy thoughts so deep
That even dreams of spring can only scold
And send us back to quilts to bring on sleep.

The eyes of winter understand the pain.
They sense the inner wounds that pinch and tear,
That spread out wide to show the fleshy stain
That swallows whole all reason and despair.

The eyes of winter watch the frosty haze
That crackles as it seeks the long lost light
And asks the silver mist to wrap short days
In cashmere threads of coverlets so white.

The darkened eyes of winter look in fear
As they approach the coffin of the year.

Take this hope of a day

Take this hope of a day
That smells of snowdrops and gardenias,
That feels the pulse,
That speaks of bliss.
Catch this joy
That holds,
That cradles,
That hugs
The loneliness of the other
And colors the sky with morning.
Learn the hands.
Follow the feet.
Find the smile.
Take this hope of a day
That hums a name,
That walks the miles,
That caresses the earth.
Honor this love
That sings the song,
That eats the bread,
That heals the ache,
That greets this hope of a day.

three...

Stones and Hard Edges

In this desert landscape,
      there are so many stones, so many rocks.
Gray-brown gravel, boulders of burnt umber.
No grass. No trees with green leaves.
Just stones and parched rocks.
Not raised by desert spaces and hard edges,
I know soft grass and rolling pastures,
Lilacs and azaleas.
Bendable birches nurture me.
This desert is sharp and hard,
      unflinching, rigid.
No soft earth
      to come up unannounced between my toes.
Just dry stones and hard edges
      to trip me,
      to break my bones.

Fragments of Scotch

With shrapnel in his legs,
      he limped and hopped, but uttered no complaints..
His legs got numb, and soon he had just one.
He favored scotch, but bourbon was fine, too.
The ice was fresh; the glass was always full.
He scoffed at drinks with fancy, funny names.
No umbrellas, no sticks of fruit for him.
Just scotch or bourbon. Just those for men, he said.
Bits of iron splinters, fragments, shards,
      pierced his leg like barbs from a deadly game of darts.
High velocity debris, that's what he called it.
Projectiles, particles caused the wounds.
Injury to skin, muscle, bone.
Surgeons scraped away dead tissue,
      but still some bits of shrapnel weighed him down.
In 1944, the litter bearers found him with the dead.
And still his sons refill his glass
      to keep the dead at bay.

Vestiges

In the far corner of the attic
Half hidden by Samsonite suitcases and threadbare overcoats
     hanging from rafters,
The trunk embraces the old memories loitering under the dust.
Photos, long-forgotten keepsakes, misplaced people, lost time.
Faces and places folded into the wrinkles of generations.
No names written on the backs of photos.
A black and white Kodak print of open, tilled fields
Before rubber stamp houses replaced potatoes.
A program from Rita's Dancing School,
     the Hat Box tap dance routine,
Patent leather dresses, all shiny black,
Red netting tutus peeking out beneath.
Mom was proud of those costumes.
And Betsy, now dead, sang My Funny Valentine
Wearing the flowing white dress that Aunt Virginia sewed.
And the remnant of a sixth grade history project
Assigned by Mrs. Bullis to give the boys
A chance to learn about the hard life of pioneers.
Dad was proud of that cabin,
Especially the roughness of the log-branches
Still wearing their bark.
And off behind the trunk,
A doll carriage hidden under a sheet,
Black leatherette with four big spoke wheels
     and a collapsible hood
To keep the baby out of the weather.
That was a Christmas present from Grandpa
Whose fingers were stained mahogany
From 40 years in the furniture factory
Polishing tables and buffing buffets.
And from the trunk's depths,
Three cobalt blue perfume bottles,
Topped with fluted silver caps,
Surrender the sweetly lingering fragrance
     of *Evening in Paris*.
But we never went to France.

Carry-Bags

My carry-bags are ready.
They hang on door knobs and on the back of my wheelchair.
They are hooked over hangers and floor lamp stands.
The bags are everywhere.
Ghosts and grime outline the logos and stitches of each bag,
And in some you will still find petals and conversations.
Food Giant totes and a Trader Joe canvas carry-all,
Crinkly plastic bags that once held
      onions and potatoes and lemon yogurt.
I cannot go traveling without the red one embossed
  with tiny white sheep and one black sheep,
The one from the gift shop
    at the Royal Botanical Gardens at Kew,
The one that has held crochet hooks and soft skeins of yarn,
Train tickets and hex wrenches.
The bag from Kew Gardens holds my walking days
  and thirty years of my life before MS.
The sturdy purple bag with a zipper top
  is the one I use now for air travel.
The handle of that one fits over my head and around my neck
So my hands are free to roll and wheel
And hold the dog's carrier on my lap.
That purple bag came from a pharmaceutical company,
A free thank-you gift for my prescription business.
But the red and white sheep bag is priceless;
It cost everything I had.

Riding the Roof's Ridge

We climbed to the ridge of the roof.
The rain greased our footholds on the shingles.
The thunder roared its warning
 As the lightning's flashes silhouetted our faces.
We sat on the peak, legs straddling the ridgepole,
We thrust up our arms, daring, not caring,
Thumbing our teenage noses at the rules of the universe.
All the shouldn'ts and mustn'ts were lost in the thunder.
Our screams disappeared
In the voice of the rain,
On the beach and on the roof,
With the breakers and with the broken,
On the margins of the sea,
In the howl of the thunder,
And in the tears of the young rain.

et lux perpetua luceat eis

Nonna wore thick, black stockings;
Mormor wore white cotton hose;
Mom wore nylons with seams;
And now my legs are bare.

Ellis Island absorbed their footprints.
In their satchels they carried dreams and bright hopes
        and visions of the 'golden door.'
Olive-skinned Italians and light-shimmering Swedes,
        with tales in their memories of weavers and fishermen,
        stone masons and bakers,
        with recipes in their heads for gnocchi and gravlax,
        with skills in their callused
        hands for the nourishing of families.
Morfar's fingers were stained mahogany from furniture refinishing.
Nonno gathered dark purple grapes from the arbor to make grappa.
And now furniture arrives in cardboard boxes,
        and wine comes in bottles with screw tops.

Their new country heard their songs and their prayers.
Mass and hymns gave order to Sunday mornings.
'Ave Maria' and 'Salve Regina'
"Rock of Ages" and "A Mighty Fortress is our God"
Sunday School meant memorizing "Jesus Loves Me"
        wearing Sunday best
        complete with patent leather Mary Janes.
Mass meant sitting quietly on wooden pews,
        squeezed between fleshy grown-ups.
And now a learner's permit comes before First Communion
        and Sunday mornings are for sleeping late.

Their new streets smelled of their old countries,
        aromas gathered like bouquets
        from dinners simmering all day
        and finally calling the family home.
Savory oregano and dill sank into the heart's core.

Lovely cardemom-scented 'lussekatt,'
    sun-colored saffron buns baked for Santa Lucia Day.
Panettone's yeasty Christmas sweetness
    crowded with citron and raisins,
    and peel of orange and lemon.
Beefy gravy for pot roast
    and hearty tomato sauce enveloping mounds of ravioli.
Pea soup thick on the tongue
    and minestrone chunky
    with potatoes and onions and beans.
And now mothers go to work
    and children go to soccer practice and the mall
    after eating take-out dinners in silence.

Their new neighborhoods nurtured their children:
    Tenement communities with stick ball in the streets,
    Double Dutch and hop-scotch on sidewalks
        in front of aunties watching from their stoops.
And now suburban lawns mark fenced lines for dogs and children.
    Towns fill with ticky-tacky houses
    with cars in every driveway.
Old neighborhoods died with the old languages
    that parents did not pass on.
They said, "You're American now;
    no need for the old ways."

Words Unraveled

The key, rusty filigree flaking away
Like withered petals in a storm of marigolds.
The trunk, smooth, wide, oaken boards
Pegged together to hold its dreams.
The silken gowns, rumpled and stained,
Infused with the scent of roses long dead.
The mirror, framed with the flattened imprints of golden yarrow,
A ring of Knight's Milfoil from long ago.
The book, its dark leather cover scratched by nights
Of solitary reading in a bed of cushions and counterpanes.
The letter, its edges frayed like ripped satin,
With words unraveled by a final goodbye.

Now the Back Page

I search the back page of the morning paper
for the latest casualties,
no longer put on the front page of our 10-page daily.
Our small town folk would cancel their subscriptions.
Tragedy's not supposed to come home any more.
That was years ago when they were just starting out.
They were 18, maybe 19,
and mom and dad were sobbing.
Those names meant something:
a hole in the heart and an empty place at the table,
hand-me-downs used for rags,
a jalopy rusting away in the yard.
The high school would have had a memorial at graduation.
But now the paper describes Baghdad and Fallujah.
Used to be Dunkirk, Anzio, Stalingrad, Manila.
The weather's different.
And now the paper's back page is full.
And our coffee is growing cold.

To Sing the Children Home

He didn't wear a uniform or carry a gun.
He didn't maim or kill or aid the god of war.
No, with hymns and ancient chants, he served
      the ones who stayed behind
      to sing the children home.
In emptiness of churches,
      he felt the ghosts of long-gone worshippers
      as strains of Palestrina called them back
      to realms of recollected ritual.
And then, within a shadow of the years,
      one did come back, still wearing dog tags;
      his glory days were spent.
A friend.
This death released the grief for martyrs past.
For this one he would play
      so the ghosts could sing,
      so the young could rest in everlasting arms,
      so the mothers could endure the empty pews,
      so the fathers could return to work,
      though railing at the God they could not see.
He practiced, and he played.
And when his fingers stopped,
      when organ pipes were still,
He wept.

The High School Memorial Reunion

They won't be there to reunite.
In yearbook pictures they wore white,
Duck tail haircuts, pegged leg pants,
And smiles wide enough to dance
Away the DJ sock-hop night.

Remember Marty, he could write.
And Sal and Carol, they were tight.
And others, too, who've passed, by chance.
They won't be there.

The girls wore sweaters, fitted, quite.
Janet, Ann, and Donna, bright
Enough to know that wilful glance
That said, "Come on." "Perchance."
And though they said, "No thanks," tonight
They won't be there.

No Ripeness There

He said goodbye.
No sorrow, no regret, no pain, just goodbye.

What happened to commitment?
Throwaway relationships like bald tires sinking in a river.
Years melted into twilight shadows.
Time faded into yellowed newsprint chronicles.
Rehearsed dialogue forgotten on opening night.
Lear's Fool was dead, more sinned upon than sinning.

The pain was searing, red-hot, aching, throbbing.
Broken life, token living.
Forsaken,
Dumped like an empty oil drum,
Thrown away like gnawed-on ribs,
Snake skin left among the rocks,
Abandoned like Anne of Cleves
        to the Tower of self-doubt.
No ripeness there.

Rolling Backwards

I rolled backwards and heard someone warn,
"Hey, watch where you're going!"
as if I had eyes in the back of my head.
Well, you never know.
I considered the possibilities.
Maybe I could grow new eyes that would peek
from behind blonde-brown strands,
hair that had never been colored,
always freshly coiffed.
Making a five-point turn, I found a new view,
different belt buckles, different waistlines.
Glasses dripped drops of Merlot;
Cracker crumbs fell on my arm.
Above my head conversations flourished.
Undertones of last night's dinner party, the vacation of a lifetime,
the importance of having a retirement plan.
"Whose voice is that?" I wondered to myself,
as somewhere in the stratosphere, someone said, "And I just had
the door jambs refinished."
"What about living in a tent?" I mused.
Wide doorways, expansive walls, room for all.
I rolled backwards again,
bumping into experience,
saluting the spirit of my life.

four...

Dottie's Diner

The menus on the door entice,
No thought for price
Or healthy fare.
Just beefsteak rare
And mashed potatoes, cream pies, food
That soothes, not stewed
Or canned, but made
With love, displayed
On Homer Laughlin plates with pride
And skill. Beside
The dish, a bill,
And much goodwill.

On the tip of my tongue

Sometimes it is right there, on the tip of my tongue,
And I just can't shove it off the edge.
It hangs there with both hands
Squeezing my taste buds so hard they pop.
But the word won't come out.
All I can say is "You know, that thing that cuts the grass"
Or "that jar with the white spread for sandwiches."
I have come up with some doozies of definitions.
I have my own dictionary,
And it keeps getting bigger and bigger.
Those recalcitrant words can be so noncompliant
That sometimes I have to send them to a time-out.
Like that word for the pain in your side
      when you run too hard.
Or the word for the feeling of having been tickled too much.
And the word for the itch in the middle of your back
      that you can't reach.
That word for the word that you cannot dislodge
From the electric misfiring of synapses and sounds.
I often think that somewhere on my tongue
There is a conference of stubborn words talking to each other,
And the lexicon that's used to enhance their deliberations
Would, as they say, make a sailor blush.
And the smiles continue as I search for the word
That says what I mean; you know,
That thing on the end of the hose
      where the water comes out
And the place on the cell phone that lists the people you call
And the way that the dog hops around on two legs.
And then, again, maybe there just isn't a word for that.
Maybe sometimes you just have to describe something
The way you see it.   Or you just have to make up words
Like Lewis Carroll did in "Jabberwocky."
I think I'd like to gyre in this brillig day
And have a picnic of liverwurst sandwiches
And you, know, those small, crispy sour things.

The Game

As every mother makes the choice
To yell full voice
To every kid
Whoever slid
Toward a base in a dusty cloud,
"I am so proud !"
The pitcher throws
The highs and lows
The balls and strikes and walks and outs
Until the shouts
Are flying free,
"Ahead by three!"

Battle Zucchini

As the garden teems with plump, green cylinders gone wild,
The most seasoned chef is challenged
In Battle Zucchini.
Armed with a paring knife, sharp and steadfast,
Like a silver sword ready to do battle,
And wearing her blue jeans, sturdy as chain mail,
The chef approaches one of six squash hills.
The sun glints off the fruits' shiny skin
As droplets of dew drip to the earth.
Demeter would be proud of the bounty here displayed
And would give her green colors to the Warrior Chef.
Not ambrosia nor the acorns of Circe,
But zucchini would be the new food of the gods.
The chef chose three sleek squash for the sacrifice.
 Placed them in a colander,
And marched into the kitchen to wash them clean.
She prepared the mandolin
for the smooth skinned beauties.
And sliced them into paper thin rounds.
Ladling olive oil into the skillet
and adding hearty chopped onions,
She cooked and stirred.
Then she put in the zucchini and chopped tomatoes.
Sprinkle in lovely basil, salt and pepper;
Then taste and see!
Oh, yes. That is food for the gods.
She returned to the garden with her paring knife.
And filled the garden basket
with all the zucchini she could find.
Into the kitchen for the squash showers and slicing.
And how much sauce could the chef make?
"Enough," she said, "Enough."
The legions would be filled!

Myrtle the Turtle

Yertle the Turtle* was more famous than me,
For I'm just a turtle named Myrtle, you see.
Dr. Seuss formed Yertle, the King of the Pond,
And my mommy made me with a wave of her wand.

To be King of the land was Yertle's desire
But instead he fell down in the mud and the mire.
I'm not a king nor a prince nor a queen,
But I am a turtle all lovely and green.

I'm Myrtle, a turtle, a friend for your day.
We'll sing out with laughter; we'll jump rope and play.
My shell is all velvety, soft like the moss;
Not hard like a box or a ball you can toss.

My eyes are wide open and round so I spot
The colors of morning and noon when it's hot.
My belly is plump and filled with good food
The kind that your mother chopped up and then stewed.

I live in a turtle house down by the lake
With my brothers and sisters and even a snake.
When I go forward, I stick my neck out
And the rest of my body just follows, no doubt.

I travel quite slowly around every nook
To visit the creatures who live in the brook.
They all give a greeting, a nod, or a call.
I can hear each of them, the big and the small.

I'm Myrtle the Turtle and this is my hope:
To keep moving onward, right up the slope,
So all of my being will help me be wise
And kind to the creatures, no matter their size.

I'm Myrtle the Turtle and I have a voice
To tell all my friends that we have a choice
To be friends with all who live in the pond
No matter their hair color, green, red, or blonde.

*Yertle the Turtle, Dr. Seuss, Random House, 1958

Sorry

I missed the gecko.
It was faster than my three-wheeled scooter.
I saw it skitter into the mulch beside the house.
The three-inch grasshopper was not so lucky.
I didn't see it until it was too late.
Like a deer in the headlights,
It didn't move.
I am sorry.

Abigail, the Dueña of the Frigidaire

She perched on top of the vintage 1950 Frigidaire
Just inside the door to the apartment.
She kept watch, a Siamese cat to be reckoned with.
Every visitor had to pass Abigail's inspection
    to be let into her space.
Her deep blue eyes could penetrate everyone's heart.
Abigail could talk a mean streak and could divulge secrets
    that had been hidden in the closet for months.
When spoken to, she answered questions directly.
She knew what she was talking about.
When I met the love of my life,
Abigail took some time to decide if he was worthy
    to share her life and mine.
She jumped up to her perch every time he came to visit.
She pulled up tall; her pointed ears almost touched the ceiling.
She paced around the top of the Frigidaire.
Displaying her muscular elegance.
Then one time, she stretched and extended herself
Along the edge of the Frigidaire.
She purred and swatted my visitor's head.
With that, my fiancé passed Abigail's inspection.
But good night kisses were still monitored
By Abigail, the Dueña of the Frigidaire.
And after my love and I were married,
Abigail gave up her perch on the Frigidaire
To take up her new place of honor
    between the pillows on our bed.

Wonder Where They Went

The kids grow up before you know,
From crawling babes to teens who drive,
From onesies cute and cheeks aglow,
To platform heels and brains that strive.

From crawling babes to teens who drive
They're off to find their inner call.
On platform heels and brains that strive,
They've changed to walking cool and tall.

They're off to find their inner call.
While parents wonder where they went,
They've changed to walking cool and tall.
Their growing up we can't prevent;

While parents wonder where they went
They change from children to adults.
Their growing up we can't prevent
We just must wait to see results.

They change from children to adults.
We try to hold and not let go,
But we must wait to see results.
The kids grow up before you know.

The Diva

A diva known only as Flossie
Had a penchant for doing things saucy.
She sang her high C's
While doing striptease,
Blowing kisses from lips red and glossy.

They Live

I pile; I do not file.
And that is why
My room is dense with reams of paper,
Full of long-abandoned couplets, hints of poems.
Packed in paragraphs of houses,
Fields of sunflower sonnets,
Children sing, and grandmothers bake cookies.
Creatures of skin and bone, breath and pulse,
They live in piled stacks of muse-forsaken stanzas.
To destroy them would be murder.

five...

My Grandfather Had Mahogany Fingers

My grandfather had mahogany fingers
From staining tables in the furniture factory.
Red in his skin,
Maroon under his nails.
It was permanent.
My Swedish grandfather,
Born in Goteborg,
  one of the huddled masses,
  one of the tempest tossed.
His shock of thick white hair stayed with him
  to the grave.
That is how I remember him,
With white hair and mahogany fingers,
As he jounced me on his foot
As he sang
      "Rheea Rheea Rhunka.
      Hadsta nea blunka,
      Vord Stata Nea"
That childhood rhyme that had no translation,
And the white hair,
And the mahogany fingers,
That had no other syntax.

Bas-relief

In my grandmother's face I see
Crinkles of children, tucks of time,
Sculpted into the rifts and gorges
Of longing and remembering
Forming chasms between body and spirit.
As I trace her face from forehead to chin
I find random ravines of births and losses,
Crevasses deepened
        by goodbyes, by joys, by deaths.
Artificial masks are surrendered.
Winter's freezes and summer's thaws
Created a countenance that recorded
Life's thousand years
        detailed by touch, look, word.
The canyons of life,
Creases of brow and cheek
        carved into bas-relief,
The wrinkles of generations.

Smoking Her Chesterfields

She sat at the vanity in the small bedroom.
The glass ashtray was filled with cigarette butts,
Probably 40 snuffed butts. The mirror was dim,
Coated with smoke and chocolate nicotine.
She leaned closer to the mirror on the wall,
A tube of red lipstick in her right hand
And a Chesterfield cigarette in the left.
Gray and brown hairs floated like miniature tails
From her hairbrush, as she exhaled
Deep puffs of smoke over the vanity.
She outlined her thinning lips with apple-red gloss
And then rubbed her lips together
To smooth out the wrinkles and fill in the cracks.
She left a red imprint on the cigarette
As she took a long, deep drag
And examined her face in the mirror.
The ash length grew on the end of the Chesterfield.
The ashes dropped on the vanity,
Mixing with the dust of powder and rouge.
She lit another cigarette
From the still-red end of the Chesterfield
Which she then snuffed in the ashtray. 41 butts.
A deep drag on the fresh Chesterfield.
A brown puff of smoke blew
    over the tails in the hairbrush.
She sat back on the vanity stool,
    her red lips quivering.
His death was not expected,
    and she was not prepared.
She had always thought she would go first.
The old 'Jack Sprat' rhyme had been their story -
He would eat no fat,
    just healthy grains, lean meat, and fruits.
She loved bacon and donuts, cream sauces and cakes.
And what had that gotten her?
The last quarter of her life to be lived alone,

Staring at the mirror
Brushing her hair
Outlining her lips
Smoking her Chesterfields.

Your Next Email

I got your email just today
And see you've moved to Southside Bay.
That's where sea and sand collide,
A great place for a getaway.

And in your note I see you tried
To find a place to stem the tide
Of indecision and the bland
Routine of life you had decried.

Your next email should be a grand
Announcement, saying that you've planned
To move again, without delay,

I See On Facebook

I see on Facebook that you moved to France.
You didn't tell me that you learned to dance
Or that you felt the rain or learned to fly.
The last I heard you wanted most to try
Your hand at writing poems of black romance.

Perhaps those verses will bring to you a chance
For admiration, not just a passing glance.
Then you will post the travels and goodbyes
I'll see on Facebook.

But now you want to change your circumstance
To show the world your knowledge, and enhance
Your rhythmic stanzas to create deep sighs
That bring from me the pensive, tear-drenched eyes
You'll see on Facebook.

The Ballad of Stitches and Schemes

The script is written; the play is cast.
The silk and satin wait.
Sketch the dress, and sew the past
With thread and stitches straight.

Her job is set; she knows the way.
Create the look of dreams.
Choose the form, the drape, the sway.
Illusions all, the schemes.

This one young, so valiant, bold;
Another, tired and gray,
And yet one more with heart so cold,
Her life in disarray.

A chain-mail suit for one so brave
While all his deeds extol.
Linsey-woolsey for the old one's grave
For soon the bell would toll.

Then this one, Anne, had seen such gloom
That she could not go on
With steady steps nor radiant bloom,
So tired of being the pawn.

The seamstress found the fabric true
To costume poor, sad, Anne.
The lovely cloth of golden hue
Would shimmer in the plan.

Anne needed such a kindly stroke
Of beauty all around.
A silken dress, a velvet cloak,
A golden band for crown.

The seamstress draped the fabric round
To show the greatest sheen.
She cut the goods and sewed the gown
So Anne would look the queen.

And next, with needle in her hand,
The cloak to show the reign,
And, finally, the golden band,
That ended all the pain.

The curtain fell on poor, sad Anne.
No more the queen attend.
The seamstress too had sewed her last
The final stitch, the end.

Lost

He will cover you with his feathers, and under his wings you will find refuge
(Psalm 91)

Masts and rigging to catch the wind,
A safe haven, protected mooring,
These have disappeared along with your smile.
Your warm ocean smell,
Your silhouette and strong shoulders,
These have gone missing.
These have vanished in squalls of weeping.
Now there is only
The hush of the wind's breath in a silent room.

I wanted to see

I wanted to see what you looked like now.
    those few strands of hair
    that you combed from left to right.
That beard, reddish-blond, Whitmanesque.
New glasses or still the horn-rimmed ones
    that said 'professor' and 'well-read.'
I expected your nose would be wide and fleshy still,
    and your eyes,
    the azure blue that mirrored your seas.
Had you taken to wearing a belt
    or did your jeans still sit way down on your hips.
I wanted to see what life had given you.
Did you have that sense of fatherhood?
Did you have that look of having achieved your purpose?
How many books had you published?
How many words had you conquered?
I wanted to see what you had become.
I wanted you to see what you had lost.

I Will Put You In A Poem

I will put you in a poem.
I will paint it khaki and blue.
The poem will show your sky and your earth.
Not a sonnet with rigid rhyme and counted meter.
Not a ballad that moans of love lost
    or train whistles fading over the miles.
Not a villanelle that measures length of lines or thoughts repeated.
No, your poem must hold your song of years,
A song that has history, love and longing.
Your poem will offer your practice schedule
    and your spirit's searching.
Your poem will describe the sandy roads you travel
    just to see what's there.
Your poem will embrace internal rhythm
That flows like a sonata of maple syrup
From one pancake to the next.
Your poem will have the sun to keep you warm
And the dark to let you sleep.
I will sing your love in a poem.
I will chant your smile in a song.
I will write your life in a fugue.
I will put you in a poem.

To See You in the Shadows

To see you in the shadows, in the mist,
I marked that scent of lilacs where we kissed.
That lingering aroma haunts my prayer.
I long for you when breezes swell the air
With lilac's heady balm. I can't resist.

Your grit and spirit live within the midst
Of deeper sorrows, but they still insist
That I should part the curtains just a hair,
To see you in the shadows.

Remembering the time you played the Liszt
Brings back the anguish of that fateful tryst.
That heady fragrance and those musings dare
To portend heartbreak; thus, I cannot bear
To see you in the shadows.

When I Have Loved Enough

When I have loved enough to keep the sun
From baking fields and setting leaves ablaze,
The heat will then just scorch and turn to dun
The brightness of the gold I want to praise.

When I have loved enough, I will have found
The light to gather into grand bouquets
To give to you, to all, with promise crowned
By sprays of loving kindness and high praise.

When I have loved enough, the wayward years
And unrelenting days that clutch and hold
To hopes, like lonely, painted souvenirs,
Will then give way to dreams my youth extolled.

When I have loved enough, I hope to see
All those who freely shared their love with me.

CPSIA information can be obtained at www.ICGtesting.com
Printed in the USA
LVOW041023180412

278147LV00003B/2/P